Things That
Make You Go

YUCK!

The Urbana Free Library

To renew: call **217-367-4057**
or go to **urbanafreelibrary.org**
and select **My Account**

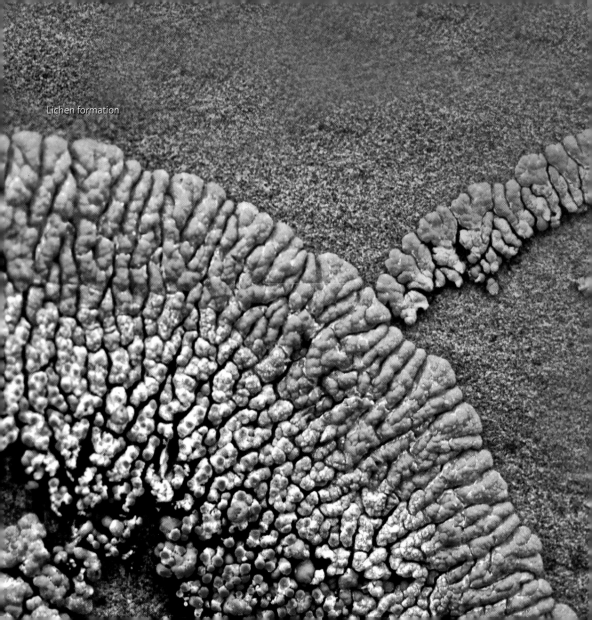
Lichen formation

Things That Make You Go

YUCK!

Odd Couples

Jenn Dlugos & Charlie Hatton

Prufrock Press Inc.
Waco, Texas

Library of Congress Cataloging-in-Publication Data

Names: Dlugos, Jenn, author. | Hatton, Charlie, author.
Title: Things that make you go yuck! : odd couples / by Jenn Dlugos and
  Charlie Hatton.
Description: Waco, Texas : Prufrock Press Inc.,
[2017] | Audience: Ages 9-12.
  | Includes bibliographical references.
Identifiers: LCCN 2016035486 | ISBN 9781618215666 (pbk.)
Subjects: LCSH: Adaptation (Biology)--Juvenile literature. | Courtship in
  animals--Juvenile literature. | Mutualism (Biology)--Juvenile literature.
  | Parasites--Juvenile literature.
Classification: LCC QH546 .D5856 2017 | DDC 578.4--dc23
LC record available at https://lccn.loc.gov/2016035486

Copyright © 2017, Prufrock Press Inc.
Edited by Lacy Compton
Cover and layout design by Raquel Trevino

ISBN-13: 978-1-61821-566-6

Printed in the United States of America.

Prufrock Press Inc.
P.O. Box 8813
Waco, TX 76714-8813
Phone: (800) 998-2208
Fax: (800) 240-0333
http://www.prufrock.com

Portuguese man-of-war

Table
of Contents

Humpback whale
with barnacles

Introduction

You're never alone. It's true for people, and for all the other organisms on our planet, too. Plants, animals, bacteria, and fungi all live their lives intermingled—sometimes with members of the same species, other times with individuals from other species. Everywhere a creature turns, there's another critter staring back. Maybe it's a friend. Or a rival. It might be interested in mooching, mating, murdering—or all of the above. Life on Earth is an endless series of relationships, and some of them get pretty complicated. It's like a soap opera. Or middle school.

Symbiosis, Feel the Closeness

When two organisms interact and at least one benefits from the situation, their relationship is called *symbiosis*. There are several types of symbiotic relationships, depending on whether both partners are being helped, hurt, or otherwise. If both organisms benefit, the relationship is called *mutualistic*—as in, everybody mutually benefits. How nice.

There are also *commensal* relationships, where one organism is helped and the other is basically unaffected. A barnacle hitching a ride on a whale doesn't hurt the whale, or particularly help it. It's only good for the barnacle, but the whale doesn't mind. Whales are cool like that.

The Dark Symbiotic Side

Not all symbiotic relationships are quite so sunny, however. *Parasitism* is another type of symbiosis, where one organism gains—by stealing food, resources, or body parts—from a "host" organism on the other side. Some species are *obligate parasites*, which means they can't survive without taking advantage of other species in this way, while others—*facultative parasites*—just do it for fun. (Actually, for a competitive survival advantage. But the sneaky little stinkers probably have fun while they're at it.)

Some scientists would add less direct relationships, like competing for resources or one animal preying on another, to the list of "one-sided" symbioses. These certainly qualify as "close interactions" between species—even if one of those interactions involves being eaten for lunch!

Keep It in the Species

When it comes to symbiosis, most people think of interspecies relationships, meaning those between individuals of two different species. But intraspecies relations—between members of the same species—can be just as tricky, or worse. After all, organisms can only reproduce within their species. Finding (and impressing and surviving) a potential mate is a very special sort of relationship. And in many species, extra-specially strange.

It Takes Two to Tango

Whether inside the species or out, every organism deals with symbiotic relationships—whether they like it or not. In the chapters ahead, we look at some of the oddest, ickiest, and weirdest couples in nature. They don't always get along. But they're stuck with each other.

A spiny ant with a herd of mealybugs.

Forest dung beetle

1 Peculiar Pals

We all have weird friends. They do things a little bit differently than most folks, but their quirks are actually what make them fun to be around. In the wild, there are many peculiar pals. Species that have no business being chummy with each other join forces to find food, secure shelter, or just try to survive. Here are some of the most bizarre buddies out there.

Do You Know Your Odd Couples?

These insects live inside a bug-eating pitcher plant.

a. Diving ants   b. Dung beetles   c. Apple aphids

Find out the answer at the end of the chapter!

The Meat-Eating Toilet

W e humans don't ask for much from a bathroom. Cleanliness? Check. Plenty of toilet paper? Double check. A toilet that won't eat us? Check plus infinity (and beyond).

The Hardwicke's woolly bat isn't nearly as discerning. When nature calls, this little bat often relieves itself inside a bug-eating pitcher plant. These plants have tall, vase-like pits filled with digestive juices ready to gobble up any insect that tumbles inside. Pitcher plants make convenient rest stops for the bat, and not just for the easy-access restroom. Bats are nocturnal, and the pitchers give them a safe and cozy area to snooze during the day. Also, bats navigate using echolocation—they send out high-frequency sounds and interpret the echoes that bounce back. Some scientists think the unusual shapes of the pitcher plants offer an echo-friendly habitat for the bat.

Oddly, the pitcher plants also benefit from being mistaken for a toilet, because the bats' feces and urine are full of nutrients the plants need for growth. When scientists analyzed plants that bats lived in, they found that more than 30% of the nutrients these meat-eating plants consumed came from bat poop and pee. We don't know about you, but if we ever get an invite to the Batcave, we are definitely *not* asking to use the bathroom.

The Bottomless Pit

Bats and pitcher plants both eat insects, but the bats keep their wings off the plants' meals. This isn't really by choice. Even if a bat wanted to steal a yummy-looking bug from the plant, the pitcher is so deep that the bat would get stuck halfway down.

Rah! Rah! Sis Boom Die!

With deadly sharks, killer whales, and stinging jellyfish, life under the sea is utterly terrifying. Fortunately, when spirits get low, there is one little crab perfectly willing to sit on the sidelines and cheer on its fellow sea critters. The pom-pom crab lives around the Hawaiian Islands and gets its name because it is literally the cheerleader of the sea.

Being small and scrumptious-looking to larger sea predators, this feisty little crab has developed a unique way to defend itself and capture its own prey. It holds a sea anemone in each claw, and waves them around like two fluffy pom-poms. While this looks absolutely ridiculous to us land dwellers, it's actually terrifying to sea critters. Anemones have stinging cells in their tentacles, and the crabs use them to stun prey or deflect a hungry predator. The anemone likely gets a perk, too. It gets to eat a little of what the crab catches, or what it can pick up as the crab carries it across the sea floor.

However, there is a tradeoff. Clutching its stinging pom-poms means that the crab can't fully use its claws to eat, so it has to shove food in its mouth using its legs. With that kind of agility, it's just a matter of time before these cheering crabs start doing cartwheels and splits.

Cloning Pom-Poms

If a crab loses its pom-pom, it can clone the one it still has. Some anemones reproduce by binary fission, meaning one anemone can literally split itself into two to form a new organism.

Does a
Sloth Poop
in the Woods?

Well, yes, it does. But it's where it poops—and how many critters care about where it poops—that's peculiar. Sloths live in tropical rainforests, and they spend most of their lives up in trees. They have slow metabolisms, which means they are about as active as, well, sloths. Except when it comes to pooping, apparently. When nature calls, these slovenly critters crawl all the way down the trees, poop, and then crawl all the way back up. Part of it is probably socialization—they hobnob with other sloths down there. But scientists from the University of Wisconsin-Madison found another possible reason that is much, much stranger.

Deadly Duty

Pooping is deadly business for sloths. Some scientists estimate that more than half of sloth deaths by predators occur when they climb down the tree to poop.

Sloth moths and algae are two organisms that live in the fur of sloths, and all three organisms may benefit each other. Female moths lay their eggs in sloth poop on the ground. When the eggs hatch, the larvae hop on the back of the sloth and hitch a ride up the tree. The moths live in the sloth's fur for protection. The algae that also live in the sloth's fur like to have the moths around, because they provide nutrients to the algae. The sloth may eat the algae to get important fatty acids in its diet. Simply by climbing down to poop, the sloths pick up moths that make the algae grow, so that the sloth can chomp on an algae salad anytime it wants. Maybe we should stick to asking if bears poop in the woods. They don't make things nearly as complicated.

The Prickliest of Pairs

Sea urchins aren't known for being "friendly." They grow long, sharp spines for protection, and use them to stick anything or anyone that gets too close. Some urchins also produce venom, which deters most brave or curious creatures who manage to survive the spines.

Crabs also have a reputation for being less-than-sociable sea neighbors. They're sneaky fighters, quick to pinch with their snapping claws, and widely known for being . . . well, *crabby*.

With those attitudes, you wouldn't expect sea urchins and crabs to get along—or even share the same stretch of ocean. But some species that live near East Africa, around

12

Southeast Asia, and in the Red Sea don't just say hello or meet up for sea coffee—they actually live together.

The carrier crab—or *Dorippe frascone* (dough-RIP-pah fras-CONE)—gets its name from a seemingly crazy thing it does. The crab uses its four rear legs to grab a spiny sea urchin, then hoists the urchin onto its back and carries it around, like some sort of stalk-eyed saltwater chauffeur.

Urchins don't generally like to be moved—or touched, or possibly even looked at. But oddly, they don't fight this crab-handling. Maybe they were waiting to hail a crab all along.

The unlikely pairing may be good for both parties. The crab is protected by the urchin's spines, as it scurries around the seabed. The urchin may benefit from being moved to new territory, where food is more plentiful—or maybe it's just along for the ride.

One Good Carry Deserves Another

Other crabs and urchins also pair up— and sometimes the roles are reversed. For instance, the tiny heart urchin pea crab— just 7 millimeters long—spends its whole life riding a red heart urchin. Several crabs may live on one urchin, as it slowly scoots along the ocean floor.

Three Amigos
of the Amazon

Caterpillars need all the friends they can get. Especially caterpillars like those of the larval form of the hairstreak butterfly *Terenthina terentia* (tare-en-THEE-nah tare-EN-tee-ah). Unlike other vulnerable caterpillars, these little wigglers don't grow spiny bristles or venom to protect against predators like birds or spiders—and in the Amazon rainforest where they live, there are plenty of both.

Happily, *Terenthina* caterpillars have found not just one friend to help them out, but two. The first is a rare and freaky parasitic plant that lives inside other plants—in this case, rainforest trees. Around October every year, hundreds of bright yellow bulbs break through the tree's bark like tiny alien pods. These are the parasite's flowers, and while scientists don't know much about them yet, the caterpillars definitely do. Those flowers are the caterpillars' favorite snacks.

That keeps the caterpillars fed, but still at risk of becoming someone else's lunch. So they've used the flowers' sugary goodness to make another friend. These caterpillars have "dorsal nectary organs" on their backs, which produce fluid rich in sugars and amino acids. Amazon ants that live on the same trees tap the caterpillars to get at the nectar; in return, the ants patrol the tree trunks, making sure nothing disturbs their sweet-tasting caterpillar pals.

Friends Forever

Scientists have found evidence that suggests this trio of chums has been working together for a very long time. When the caterpillars pupate into hairstreak butterflies, the coloring on their wings is gray—with small circles of yellow, which look very similar to the parasitic plants' flowers. The butterflies with this color pattern may have gained a survival advantage over many, many years by blending in better on trees sporting the parasitic flowers.

Diving ant

Odd Couples Trivia Answer

These insects live inside a bug-eating pitcher plant.

a. **Diving ants (correct)**
b. Dung beetles
c. Apple aphids

Pitcher plants leave most insects quaking in their exoskeletons, but diving ants actually make colonies inside the carnivorous fanged pitcher plant. The ants benefit, because they steal tasty-looking bugs from the plant for their own meals. In turn, the plants get nitrogen—which is needed for plant growth—from ants' feces and dead ant remains.

Think About It

The relationships in this chapter were all mutualistic, meaning that both organisms get a benefit from the friendship. If you and your best friend were other organisms, which ones would you be? How would you work together to benefit each other in the wild?

Norway rat

2 Give and Take (But Mostly Take)

Most of the time, it's good to have a friend. But when your "friend" is a parasitic species infecting you, you're probably better off on your own. A parasite is any organism that lives off a host and causes it harm. And while all the species in here are bad for their hosts, they all offer some unusual—and pretty disturbing—perks. Maybe these parasites are just trying to help. After all, what more can you ask for in a "friend"?

Do You Know Your Odd Couples?

Leishmania (leash-MAY-knee-ah) protozoa are parasites that cause a deadly disease in humans, but they may actually improve immunity in these host organisms.

a. Norway rats   b. Sandflies   c. Mosquitos

Find out the answer at the end of the chapter!

Sending
Worm Regards

S ometimes, one species' parasite is another species' pal. That's the case with the raccoon roundworm, *Baylisascaris procyonis* (bay-liss-ask-AIR-iss pro-see-ON-iss), which turns out to be pretty chummy with raccoons. And a nightmare for almost everyone else.

A large percentage of raccoons are infected with the roundworm species, up to 100% in some areas. Each raccoon may harbor 50 or more worms in its intestinal tract. Together, these worms can lay millions of eggs every day, which are passed out in the raccoon's poop. Oddly, the raccoons don't seem to mind any of this, and infected animals rarely show any symptoms of disease.

They're the lucky ones, however. Small animals exposed to the pooped-out worm eggs can also become infected—and the roundworm is much rougher on these hosts. Birds, squirrels, mice, rabbits, woodchucks, armadillos, and other animals suffer with the worms burrowing throughout their bodies. The roundworms tend to travel to the central nervous system, and can cause confusion, blindness, organ failure, loss of movement, coma, and even death.

Frankly, the raccoons don't mind this, either. That's because many animals that become infected with raccoon roundworm are also part of raccoons' usual diet. If the worms slow the raccoons' prey down so they're easier to catch—and the worms aren't harmful, even if raccoons eat them—it's a win-win for raccoons. And the worms. And nobody else.

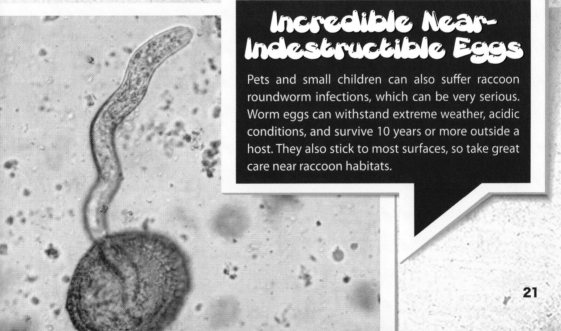

Incredible Near-Indestructible Eggs

Pets and small children can also suffer raccoon roundworm infections, which can be very serious. Worm eggs can withstand extreme weather, acidic conditions, and survive 10 years or more outside a host. They also stick to most surfaces, so take great care near raccoon habitats.

Getting a Leg (or Legs) Up

Frogs hop pretty quickly on the four legs they have. What if they had five legs, or six, or even more? Could they leap over tall lily pads in a single bound? Set new records in the Tour de Frog? Would we have to call them "jackribbits"?

As it happens, some frogs do grow extra legs, due to infection by parasitic flatworms called *Ribeiroia* (rye-beh-REE-uh). But those bonus limbs aren't all they're cracked up to be.

Most species of *Ribeiroia* have a life cycle that includes infection of three different animals: small snails that live in ponds or wetlands, frog tadpoles in those same waters, and birds that eat the frogs the tadpoles grow into. It's the second step where the frogs wind up with extra legs—and the last step where those legs work out better for *Ribeiroia* than the frogs themselves.

When the flatworms infect a tadpole, they form cysts—hard protective capsules—near the limb buds, from where the frog's legs will grow. The cysts interfere with limb development, keeping legs from growing—or making extra legs grow, in all different sizes and at weird angles.

Unfortunately for the frogs, these limbs don't work nearly as well as the usual four legs. Many infected frogs can't hop well, or move at all. That makes them sitting ducks—or sitting frogs—for birds to swoop down and eat. Which is good for *Ribeiroia*, since the birds are the worms' next host. But bad for frogs, for whom five (or six, or nine) legs are definitely not better than four.

Frog infected with Ribeiroia

A Rise in Ribeiroia

Sightings of these deformed frogs have increased dramatically since the mid-1990s. Scientists are working to understand why. Possible reasons include increased agricultural pollution, introduced species, additional parasites, and other habitat changes.

Wolbachia's Got Your Back, Girls

I f variety is the spice of life, then the bacteria family *Wolbachia* (wohl-BACK-ee-uh) is the spice of parasites. That doesn't sound nearly as appetizing, which is probably why you never see it printed on T-shirts or bumper stickers.

Don't tell that to *Wolbachia*, maybe the most variety-loving parasites around. Of all arthropod species—insects, spiders, and crustaceans—around 40% may host *Wolbachia* species. The bacteria live inside cells, including females' eggs, which pass the infection to offspring.

In many arthropod species, infection with *Wolbachia* is a problem. The bacteria can lead to death of developing males, conversion of males to females, and can block infected males from reproducing with noninfected females. As if raising a family wasn't complicated enough.

Because *Wolbachia* rely on females to spread, though, the bacteria make life easier for them—even helping females in some species to reproduce without males. Some host species, including several kinds of wasp, have been dealing with *Wolbachia* for so long, there are barely any males left. In some species, genes important for "normal" reproduction have gone silent and picked up genetic mutations. So they're now dependent on *Wolbachia* infections to reproduce, lay eggs, or possibly even survive. These bacteria can hurt, help, or anything in between.

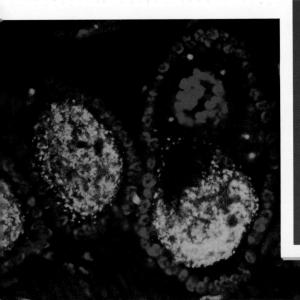

Don't Let the Bad Bugs Bite

Another potential advantage to *Wolbachia* infection is that the bacteria prevent other pathogens from taking hold. Scientists are hoping to turn this to our advantage, by introducing *Wolbachia* into mosquito species that carry dangerous diseases like dengue fever. If *Wolbachia* can infect the insects first, they may not catch diseases like dengue—or pass them on to humans.

Wolbachia bacteria, green, infect the ovaries of a malaria-transmitting mosquito.

25

Trachymyrmex fungus-growing ant

Megalomyrmex
adamsae

Betting the (Ant) Farm

You won't see blobs of sticky white fungi at your local farmer's market, but it's the latest trend in ant farming. In South America, one ant species grows colonies of fungi for food. Unfortunately, plenty of other ants want to steal the fruits of their fungal labor, most notably a parasitic ant named *Megalomyrmex symmetochus* (meg-ah-low-MER-mex sim-me-TOE-cuss).

If *Megalomyrmex* sounds like a critter that would make Godzilla quiver in his galoshes, you aren't far off. *Megalomyrmex* ants invade the fungal ants' colony, eating not only their fungi, but their offspring as well. They even snip off the wings of the fungi-growers' queen ants. Without wings, the queens are forced to become typical worker ants. Simply put, the fungi farmers quickly find themselves under new management, and their new boss is an absolute nightmare.

Mostly. There is a perk to having the *Megalomyrmex* around. They can ward off an even worse ant species—*Gnamptogenys hartmani*. When *Gnamptogenys* ants enter a colony, they don't stop at clipping off a few wings—they kill nearly every ant they see. The *Megalomyrmex* ants are much better defenders, improving the fungi-growing ants' survival from this invasion. So, if you happen to be a fungi-growing ant, your best motto might be "Live (Wing) Free or Die."

Put Your Mite Foot Forward

One of the creepiest ant parasites is a tiny mite that attaches itself to the bottom of an ant's leg to suck its hemolymph, or "ant blood." Over time, the lower part of the ant's leg falls off and the mite becomes the ant's replacement "foot."

Mite

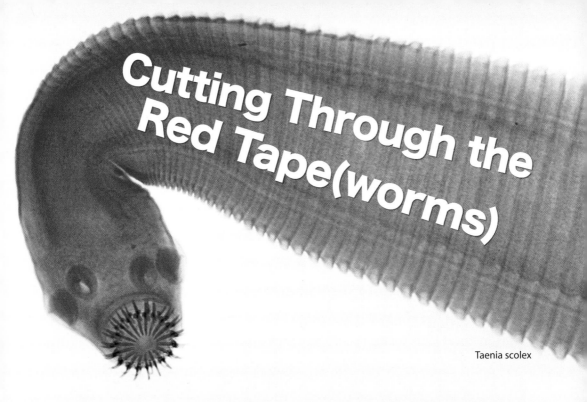

Cutting Through the Red Tape(worms)

Taenia scolex

As far as parasites go, it's hard to get grosser than the tapeworm. These creepy critters live in the digestive tract of organisms, sucking nutrients from their hosts. Some tapeworms grow to more than 50 feet in length. That's as long as a large bus, coiled up in your gut!

Tapeworms are clearly parasites, but new research suggests that having these free-loaders around may offer a few perks to some species. One study found that a species of beetle lived longer if it was infected by a tapeworm than if it wasn't. Another found that shark tapeworms filtered dangerous metals, like lead, from the shark's gut, potentially sparing the shark from their toxic effects. Some of the worms had 450 times the amount of toxic metal that the sharks did.

One of the most unusual studies showed that mice infected with tapeworms were more likely to remember that a box gave them an electric shock. The scientists first introduced the mice to the box, then gave them a chemical that triggered their immune systems. Triggering the immune system in this way usually makes mice confused, but the mice with worms showed better memory of the electric shock box than the non-wormed mice. One explanation is that the worms limited the rodents' immune responses (possibly to ensure the worm's survival).

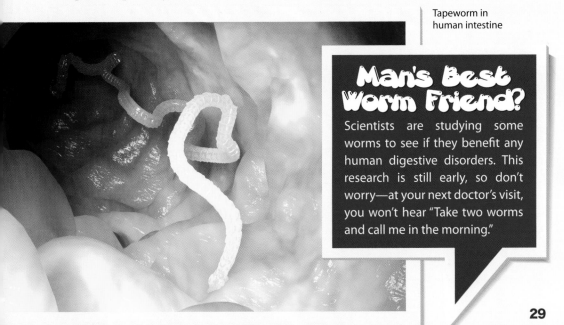

Tapeworm in human intestine

Man's Best Worm Friend?

Scientists are studying some worms to see if they benefit any human digestive disorders. This research is still early, so don't worry—at your next doctor's visit, you won't hear "Take two worms and call me in the morning."

Sandfly

Odd Couples Trivia Answer

Leishmania (leash-MAY-knee-ah) protozoa are parasites that cause a deadly disease in humans, but they may actually improve immunity in these host organisms.

a. Norway rats
b. **Sandflies (correct)**
c. Mosquitos

Several research studies showed that *Leishmania* shorten life expectancy for sandflies, one of the insects that carry this deadly parasite. However, a team of British and Brazilian researchers found an interesting perk of these parasites—they actually protected the flies from another deadly germ. The scientists exposed a bunch of sandflies to a deadly bacteria and found that the *Leishmania*-infected flies were more likely to survive.

Think About It

Nothing about the wild is black and white. Even parasites, which are known for harming their hosts, may offer a few perks to the organisms they infect. Do the perks outweigh the damage? That's for you to decide. Pretend you are a lawyer in Critter Court. The case is one of the parasites in this chapter against the host it infects. Which side would you defend? How would you plead your critter's case to the judge?

Green parrot
lovebird

3 May I Have This Dance?

Producing offspring ensures the long-term survival of a species, and every species has its own special way of attracting a mate. Some of the methods are so elaborate they put Cupid to shame. The critters in this chapter are a few of the hopeless romantics that give it their all to pop the big question and live happily ever after.

Do You Know Your Odd Couples?

This bird is called the moonwalking bird because it dances backwards to attract its mate.

a. Oxpecker   b. Lovebird   c. Manakin

Find out the answer at the end of the chapter!

Proud as a Peacock Spider

I f we had to guess which critters were the best dancers in the animal kingdom, we'd vote for spiders. With seven joints on each of their eight legs, they definitely have bodies built to "cut a rug," as your grandparents used to say. (Hopefully not *on* your grandparents' rug. No one needs a spider dance party happening on Grandma's shag carpeting.)

The tiny and colorful peacock spider is one arachnid known for its ability to bust a move for love. Intricate mating dances are common in birds and other higher organisms, but these spiders show everyone that they know how to shake a tail feather. When a male spots a female, it moves two of its legs in a rhythmic up and down motion much like an air traffic controller directing traffic. A colorful flap on its abdomen stands straight up, like the plumes of a peacock, and the spider can even do "somersaults," scampering over and under a rock or log to win the female's affection. The whole thing looks like a matinee performance of Cirque du Spider-leil.

And the male spider better hope the female digs his moves. If she doesn't, or she has already mated, she'll often eat him. So, take heed, male peacock spiders. If your lady wants to go out for dancing *and* dinner, find yourself another partner.

Every Party Is a Costume Party

A newly discovered species of peacock spider is named *Skeletorus* (skel-eh-TOUR-us), because of its black-and-white markings, which make it look just like a teeny tiny skeleton.

Love
Is in the
Pipeline

Female (left) and male (right)

Humans often turn our noses up at the gross things critters make, but we have a knack for building some pretty yucky things ourselves. Take storm sewers, for instance. We build them to control flooding and collect rain water, but the water flowing into these drains often carries dirt, grime, and pollutants from our streets and driveways. This makes storm sewers a pretty unromantic place, at least for humans. One little frog, however, may use our icky storm drains to let the whole world know he's looking for love.

Many frogs have loud mating calls, but the coqui frog on Hawaii's Big Island is one of the loudest. It gets its name from the loud "Ko Kee!" sound it makes, and residents have said that these frogs can sound as loud as a jet engine.

Mientien tree frogs live in the city of Taipei, Taiwan. It's tough for a little frog to make it on his own in the big city, but some of them find solace by hopping into the city's storm sewers. These cavernous drains probably offer protection from predators, but they also offer a romantic perk. From inside, the male frogs can make louder and longer mating calls. These frogs have 13 notes in their mating calls, and scientists found that the drains made each note 10% longer.

Scientists don't know if the frogs jump into the sewers to increase their chances of finding a mate, or if the frogs that do are more successful at wooing a female frog, but one thing is for sure—these crooning romantics are certainly not going to pipe down anytime soon.

Leading You Down the Love Garden Path

R ed velvet mites must love Valentine's Day. First of all, these tiny arachnids are bright red, like tiny Valentine hearts. Secondly, they are hopeless romantics. Of all of the crazy prom proposals on YouTube, none compare to how this little mite asks a lucky lady out on a big date.

Mites are not spiders, but they share many similarities to their web-slinging relatives. They have eight legs and some weave silk, which the males use to build elaborate love gardens to attract females. They build their gardens out of twigs, leaves, and packets of sperm, so the female can fertilize her eggs. Each male mite weaves an intricate trail of silk leading to the garden, so a female mite can follow it. When the two finally meet, the male dances for the female. If the female is taken by the male's offerings, she enters the garden.

An old 80s song claims that "love is a battlefield," which is definitely true for the red velvet mite. If the male leaves his perfectly built garden and another male finds it, the second male will ransack it, claim it as its own, and often steal the girl from the first mite. Maybe mites need to watch more romantic comedies. They clearly don't understand how love stories should end.

Birdbrained Interior Decorator

Like red velvet mites, male bowerbirds build elaborate nests to woo a female. They build their nests with flowers, nuts, shells, shiny human trinkets, and even sparkly insect feces. Now, what hopeless romantic could say no to that?

Love Is in the Air Sacs

Everybody likes balloons—even in the animal kingdom. But when a romantic Romeo out in nature wants to surprise his sweetheart with a nice balloon, he can't just go buy one at the county fair. Because animals don't have money. Or fairs. Or for that matter, counties.

So some animals make their own balloons. That includes species of frigatebirds, whose males attract potential mates not with chocolate or roses, but with balloons. During mating season, male frigatebirds gather near nesting areas and put on a show. Each male has a bright red "gular pouch"—a flap of throat skin connecting the beak to the neck, similar to a pelican's.

But frigatebird gular pouches are special. They're airtight, and the birds can inflate the sacs with air. The males do so to attract a mate, raising their beaks high in the air and proudly showing off their inflated pouches to females flying overhead. These displays can last up to 20 minutes, during which the males of some species also drum on their pouches with their beaks.

If a female lands nearby to say hello, the male and female courtship may begin. If so, the male will cover the female's eyes with his wings, so she won't be distracted by other males' gular spectacles. In the world of frigatebirds, you keep your eyes on your own balloons.

Love Nose No Bounds

Frigatebirds aren't the only animals pitching woo with balloons. Male hooded seals actually have two pouches—one on top of the snout (usually black) and another (typically pink) inside the nose. Both sacs are connected to the nasal membranes. Seals inflate the pouches atop their heads to show aggression, but blow up their "nostril sacs"—which bob up and down and can make various noises—to attract females during mating season. How could a girl resist?

Polly Want a Kisser?

There are many different kinds of kisses. There's the "good-night kiss," the "peck on the cheek," and the "give Aunt Sadie a kiss for knitting your birthday sweater," to name a few. Then there are romantic kisses, smooches shared by people in love. Romantic kissing is found in about half of human cultures, has been practiced for eons, and as a species we're pretty good at it.

Among other animals, however, romantic kissing isn't nearly so common. A few species of monkeys kiss for love, and that's about it—except for the white-fronted parrot (also known as white-fronted Amazon or spectacled Amazon parrot). Males and females in this species kiss mouth-to-mouth as part of their mating behavior. But we wouldn't say they've exactly got the hang of it.

That's because the "kissing" these parrots do ends differently than most kissing, romantic or otherwise. The parrot pair begin by locking beaks and touching their tongues together. But after a few minutes of this, the male breaks form—by vomiting into the female's mouth. Talk about an embarrassing first date.

It sounds awfully gross, but among parrots even this sort of "kissing" is a sign of affection. Many birds regurgitate food for others—think of a mother bird feeding young in the nest—so in this case, the male parrot is simply offering a gift to the female. A gift of food. Already prechewed. How sweet. Remind us not to kiss any white-fronted parrots. Just in case.

Just Grin and Parrot

White-fronted Amazon parrots (species *Amazona albifrons*, or am-eh-ZOH-nah AL-beh-frons) live in Mexico and Central America, can learn 30-40 different sounds, and reach 40 years of age or more. Though a bit of a challenge, some experienced bird lovers keep them as pets.

43

Red-capped
male manakin

Female manakin

Odd Couples Trivia Answer

This bird is called the moonwalking bird because it dances backwards to attract its mate.

    a.   Oxpecker

    b.   Lovebird

    c.   Manakin (correct)

The red-capped manakin has a mean set of moves to attract a lady. It does the Electric Slide, gliding side-to-side and even backward on a branch. If that isn't enough of a spectacle, it makes noises to catch the attention of the female and to warn other male birds to stay away.

Think About It

The animals in this chapter can move freely, so they can go out and search for a mate. But what about organisms that can't move at will? How about mushrooms and other fungi? Or green plants? How do they reproduce? Do a little sleuthing on your own to find out the answer!

Chilean rose
tarantula

4 Deadly Duos

Sometimes love hurts. But it's usually not deadly, unless you're one of the poor species in this chapter. Reproduction is important to the survival of the species, but these organisms haven't quite mastered the "survive" part. These diabolical daters are so gung-ho about producing offspring that they are literally dying to mate.

Do You Know Your Odd Couples?

Some female spiders eat the male after mating, which often provides nourishment for the eggs. These male spiders, however, are known for eating certain females.

a. Brown widow spiders

b. Wolf spiders

c. Chilean rose tarantulas

Find out the answer at the end of the chapter!

Please Don't Bring Us Some

Figgy Pudding

Fig tree pollination is a really sticky situation. Most flowering plants make big, colorful blossoms that act like neon signs to bumblebees and other pollinators, but the petals of fig tree flowers are trapped inside their sticky, oozy, and non-neon figs. Fortunately, fig trees have a mutual—if highly disturbing— relationship with the tiny fig wasp that takes care of this problem.

These wasps start their lives by hatching out of eggs inside of figs, and they must fly to another fig to lay their eggs. When the eggs hatch, the male wasps are blind and wingless. They mate with the females and die shortly after, never leaving the fig they were born in. The winged females do manage to wiggle their way out of the sticky fig eventually, coating themselves with fig pollen in the process. They fly to another tree and burrow inside a new fig to lay their eggs. It's a tight squeeze, and the fig often rips the female's wings off, trapping her inside. The worst part is that she might not be able to lay her eggs. Some fig species have both male and female flowers on the same plant, but others have separate sexes. For these figs, the wasps need the structures inside of male figs for their eggs, but they can't tell the two apart from the outside. If the female wasp ends up inside a female fig, she'll die inside without laying her eggs. But she will deliver pollen to the female fig, so the plant can reproduce.

Wasp Pollination of Figs

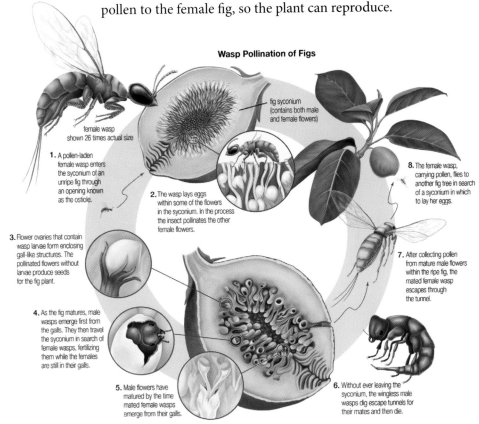

female wasp
shown 26 times actual size

fig syconium
(contains both male
and female flowers)

1. A pollen-laden female wasp enters the syconium of an unripe fig through an opening known as the ostiole.

2. The wasp lays eggs within some of the flowers in the syconium. In the process the insect pollinates the other female flowers.

3. Flower ovaries that contain wasp larvae form enclosing gall-like structures. The pollinated flowers without larvae produce seeds for the fig plant.

4. As the fig matures, male wasps emerge first from the galls. They then travel the syconium in search of female wasps, fertilizing them while the females are still in their galls.

5. Male flowers have matured by the time mated female wasps emerge from their galls.

6. Without ever leaving the syconium, the wingless male wasps dig escape tunnels for their mates and then die.

7. After collecting pollen from mature male flowers within the ripe fig, the mated female wasp escapes through the tunnel.

8. The female wasp, carrying pollen, flies to another fig tree in search of a syconium in which to lay her eggs.

Bee Mine
(or Die Trying)

L ove is a bee-autiful thing, except if you're a Dawson's burrowing bee. Then love is a bee-hemoth dose of bee-zerk. Dawson's burrowing bees are some of the largest bees on Earth, reaching nearly one inch in length. When these big buzzers mate, it's a battle to the death.

As the name suggests, these bees start their lives in underground burrows, where they live until they are fully formed adults. The adult males emerge first and wait for the female bees to arrive. When the first female emerges, the males jump on top of her, and the battle begins. The males sting, bite, and even kill each other for a chance to mate with the female. It's rare to see such brutality against one's own species, but the stakes are quite high. Each female will usually only mate once, so males fight to pass on their genes. By the end, the mating area is covered with dead male bees. Female bees are also among the dead, casualties caught in the crossfire of the great mating war.

After mating, each female digs a burrow for her eggs. All the burrows are close together, but there is no queen bee here—every bee is on her own. The females die soon after closing up their burrows, and all remains quiet until the next generation emerges and the battle begins again.

Victory for the Little Guys

During the mating battle, the biggest and most aggressive males get the most mates, but smaller male bees, called *minors*, have an interesting strategy. Instead of going into battle, they wait on the edges of the mating ground in hopes that a female manages to make it out of the brawl without mating.

Cupid's Arrow Is as Slow as a Snail

W e've all known a backstabber. These phony pals are nice to your face, but the second you turn your back, they start saying nasty things about you. Snails feel our pain, because they are some of the fiercest backstabbers (and everywhere-else stabbers) in the wild.

Many snails have both male and female organs. This is great for reproduction, because any two snails can theoretically meet up and mate. Unfortunately, mating involves stabbing each other with spear-like structures known as love darts. Love darts are not reproductive organs—they do not contain sperm or eggs—and for a long time, scientists had no idea what purpose they served. After much research, scientists now think being stabbed by the dart increases the chances that the stabber's sperm will successfully fertilize the stabbee's eggs.

As you'd probably expect, being stabbed by a giant spear comes with a few risks. In some studies, stabbed snails did not survive as long or reproduce again as quickly as the snails that avoided being pierced. Also, snails have very simple vision, so they're terrible aims. A stabbed snail could end up with a dart sticking out of almost anywhere—its neck, its butt, or right out of its head like a unicorn. Sort of makes the occasional pimple seem a lot less embarrassing, doesn't it?

No Dart for You

A snail does not have darts when it mates for the first time. Love darts only develop in snails' bodies after a snail successfully mates once.

Love Me to Death

S ometimes, finding love isn't everything; it's the only thing. And also the final thing.

That's how it works for males in *Antechinus* (an-TECK-uh-nuss) species, small shrew-like marsupials living in the forests of Australia and New Guinea. Females may live up to 2–3 years, but the lifespan of most male *Antechinuses* is less than a year. Why? Blame it on love.

Antechinus males mature within months, in plenty of time for the annual mating season. Each August or September (winter in the southern hemisphere), the males prepare for an intense few days of frantically finding partners, mating, and fighting with other males who have similar ideas. Each animal has a lot at stake—namely, passing on its genes to future generations—so the males go all-out in their search for love. That includes producing huge amounts of hormones like testosterone, skimping on vital bodily functions, and even shutting down their immune systems. All the energy they can muster goes toward mating.

But this one-track *Antechinus* mind costs the males dearly. Soon after the mating period, the increase in stress hormones and their weakened immune systems do them in, and all of the males die off, before any of the babies are born. Talk about a stressful first date.

The good news is that half the babies born will be male, and they'll keep the species going for another year. But they'd better be quick. In *Antechinus*, you really *have* to hurry love.

More Marsupials to Love

Many *Antechinus* species live in remote areas, and as those have been explored in recent years, more species have been found and identified. Of the 15 known *Antechinus* species, four have been classified since 2012, and scientists expect to find more species hiding in the forests.

The Tricky-Picky Spider

A girl knows what she likes. In Australian redback spiders, what the girls like is attention, and maybe a snack. And if they don't get enough attention, they definitely get the snack.

In this case, the "attention" comes from male redback spiders, which are 50–100 times smaller than females. At that size, romantic redbacks have to be creative to impress a lady. Males may spend hours doing a courtship dance in a female's web, which involves plucking at threads and drumming on her abdomen. It can be a long process—but there's a good reason for that.

Female redbacks are cannibals—they often eat the male after mating, or even during. If a male courts a female for less than 100 minutes, he's more likely to be eaten prematurely. That lowers his chance of passing on genes, so it's in his best interest to make an effort to impress her.

(Or in his genes' best interest, at least. He's likely getting eaten, either way.)

The game changes when there's competition for a lady redback's affection, however. If a small male and a large male are competing, the smaller one usually rushes in, well before 100 minutes—and is promptly eaten. The larger male may dance for longer, with greater success.

But if two spider suitors are the same size, one may still try to mate without performing a "long" dance. But in this case, the female is less likely to eat him prematurely. Scientists can't say why—maybe she has trouble telling the two apart. Or maybe she's saving room for dinner.

The Old Spider Switcheroo

Small male redbacks have it tough, but they do have a trick up their spider sleeves. Once one male performs a "long" courtship dance, other males—even little ones—can try to mate with the same female with less risk of being eaten early on.

Female wolf spider
with babies

Close-up of a
female wolf spider

Odd Couples Trivia Answer

Some female spiders eat the male after mating, which often provides nourishment for the eggs. These male spiders, however, are known for eating certain females.

a. Brown widow spiders
b. Wolf spiders (correct)
c. Chilean rose tarantulas

Because females lay the eggs, it seems like eating the female would lower a spider species' chance of survival. Yet, some male wolf spiders do eat the female when they come together to mate. Researchers found that they are more likely to eat females that have mated before or have poor body condition, possibly ensuring that the youngest and healthiest females have a better chance at successfully mating.

Think About It

We often hear that black widow spiders and praying mantises kill their mates, but is every date a deadly one? Actually, no. Many males of both species survive after mating to live another day. Can you think of any other "facts" we hear about animals that may not be completely accurate? Research them and find out the answers! Here are a few to get you started.

- » Do cats always land on their feet?
- » Do ladybugs actually grow a new spot every year?
- » Are bats completely blind?

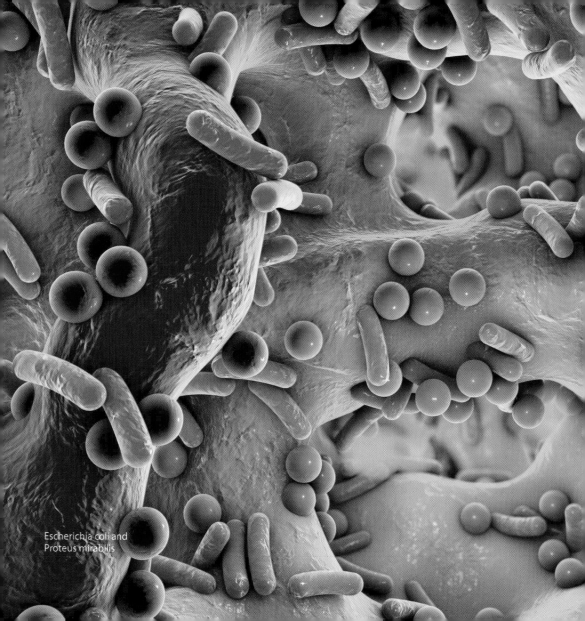

Escherichia coli and
Proteus mirabilis

5 You Complete Me

Although most species get by on their own, a few need a little help from their friends—and vice versa. In these mutual multiorganism mingles, it's hard to tell where one species ends and the other begins, but neither codependent critter could survive without that shoulder—or wing, or tentacle, or flagellum—to lean on.

Do You Know Your Odd Couples?

Gut flora is the name for:

a. all the microorganisms that live in an animal's intestines.
b. a type of flower that causes stomachaches in humans when eaten.
c. a tiny parasite that replaces the stomach of an organism with its own stomach.

Find out the answer at the end of the chapter!

Tube lichen

Common orange lichen

Common orange lichen

Cup lichen

I'm Lichen
Our Chances
Together

Beard lichen

Devil's matchsticks lichen

Wolf lichen

Antelope Island lichen

If you've ever walked through a forest, you've probably seen lichens (LYE-kins). They show up as crusty flat patches of color on trees and rocks, shrubby masses on the ground, and leafy, scaly, or hairy growths all over the woods. You'll also find lichens in the tropics, the Arctic, and the desert. Basically, a lichen grows pretty much wherever it wants, in whatever shape it wants, and in whatever color it wants. And good luck trying to get it to finish its homework.

Many people think a lichen is a plant, but it's actually a "composite organism" made from members of two species—one a fungus and the other algae or bacteria (or rarely, both). The algae (or bacteria) are surrounded by layers of fungus, like a sandwich. (We don't recommend eating most lichens; few are poisonous, but they taste about as good as they sound.)

The lichen arrangement works for both species, because they both do something the other can't. The fungus provides support and structure for the algae to grow, while the algae or bacteria use photosynthesis to convert sunlight into nutrients, which feeds the fungus. They may not be "two great tastes that taste great together," but lichens seem to get along just fine.

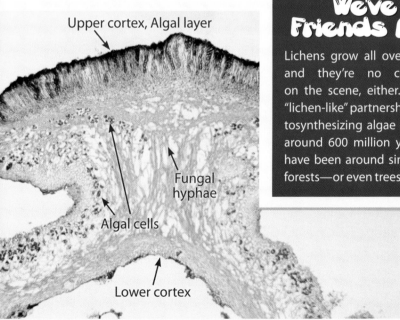

Upper cortex, Algal layer

Fungal hyphae

Algal cells

Lower cortex

We've Been Friends for Years

Lichens grow all over the planet today—and they're no composite-come-lately on the scene, either. Fossil evidence of a "lichen-like" partnership of fungus and photosynthesizing algae or bacteria goes back around 600 million years. So, lichens may have been around since before there were forests—or even trees—for them to grow in.

Two Genomes Are Better Than One?

You don't always need two species to make a dependent pair. Occasionally, a genetic hiccup creates two separate genetic codes in a single individual. Your genetic material—the DNA that makes you "you"—is called your genome. Genomes are like noses—everybody has one, and each is unique, different from anyone else's. But what if you had *two*?

(Genomes, that is. Not noses. Nobody wants two noses; your sunglasses would never fit.)

It turns out, some rare individuals called *mosaics* and *chimeras* do have two genomes. Most animals grow from a fertilized egg—but mutations early in development can give an individual different genomes in different cells (a mosaic), or two eggs can fuse together, mixing cells with different genomes (a chimera). As the animal grows, some cells get one genome; other cells get a different genome. Chimeras and mosaics can occur in plants, too.

Often, it's not easy to tell a chimera or mosaic from a single-genomed individual. It's not like checking for a second nose, after all. But sometimes the genomes code for different color skin, fur, eyes, or even different genders. Individuals may show differences in patches—or split right down the middle. These splits have been seen in people, dogs, cats, rabbits, cattle, birds, and other species. But so far, no chimeric double noses.

A New Heart Beats as Two

Chimerism usually occurs via egg fusion—but there's another way people (and some animals) may become chimeric: organ transplants. If an individual receives a kidney, liver, or heart from a donor, for instance, the cells in those organs will have a different genome. If the transplanted tissue is bone marrow, it can even change the recipient's blood type.

I'm OK, You're Acacia

You wouldn't want to disturb an African acacia (uh-CAY-shuh) tree. Not because the tree will bite—acacias actually have fewer natural defenses against interlopers or parasites than most trees. But acacias keep armies of defenders nearby, in the form of ant colonies. The trees give the ants a place to live and nourishment from sap. In return, the ants fiercely defend the tree against leaf-eating animals, invading insects, and humans wandering too close to the trunk. And a word of warning: the ants *do* bite. A lot. And hard.

But the acacia-ant friendship goes deeper than that. In addition to sap (or "nectar"), the acacias also produce "food bodies" rich in nutrients that the ants need. And a recent study shows that the ants may help to keep the trees healthy—bacteria that live on ants' legs produce substances that kill microscopic plant pathogens. The ants are like

little crawly swabs constantly trailing antiparasite juices up and down the tree.

So the ants get free lunches, and the trees get protection from invaders as big as giraffes all the way down to single-celled pathogens. It's no wonder these two species are BFFs.

On the Other Ant Hand . . .

There is one aspect of this relationship that's a little less friendly. Generally, ants can choose where to live and what to eat. But ants in an acacia colony don't have that luxury. That's because most trees have sap rich in a sugar called *sucrose*, and this sucrose is where ants eating the sap would get energy. But acacia sap has no sucrose—and on top of that, contains an enzyme that knocks out ants' ability to digest sucrose. So once ants have tasted acacia nectar, they can't feed from other trees. They're locked in with their new best "friend," the acacia tree.

Old War Buddies

To any experienced sea critter, the Portuguese man-of-war looks terrifying. It looks like a jellyfish and has long, stinging tentacles that spread up to 50 meters in length. But unlike the jellyfish, which is a single organism, the Portuguese man-of-war is a siphonophore (sigh-FON-oh-fore), a name given to colonies of organisms that work together as one unit.

Siphonophores are a weird bunch, because they challenge our definition of organism. You are a single human organism made up of trillions of cells. Your cells are not separate organisms—they are just the building blocks that stick together to form you. However, the tiny critters that make up the Portuguese man-of-war each have properties that make them unique organisms, but they join together to function like one organism.

The organisms that make up the Portuguese man-of-war are called *zooids* (ZOO-oyds), and each type of zooid has its own job. There are zooids for floatation, capturing prey, digesting food, and reproduction. Scientists are still not clear how the different zooids communicate with each other, but given those 50-meter tentacles, there's an awful lot of mass texting going on.

Saving the Sting

The sting of the Portuguese man-of-war is extremely painful, and the tentacles can deliver a nasty sting even after the colony dies. But there is one sea critter that is not afraid of its sting. The blue dragon sea slug eats the man-of-war's tentacles, and stores them in its body to use as a defense against its own predators.

It's Easy Being Green

No matter how busy our day is, every so often we have to stop and smell the rosemary. And basil. And thyme. Preferably if it's all sprinkled on a turkey sandwich with melted cheese. Animals need to eat food, so their bodies have energy. Plants and algae don't have that problem, because they make their own energy from the sun through photosynthesis. Amazingly, one little animal—a sea slug named *Elysia chlorotica* (ee-LEES-ee-uh klor-OTT-eh-kuh)—has figured out a way to tap into its inner plant.

Chloroplasts are parts of plant cells that allow photosynthesis to happen, because they contain chlorophyll. Animal cells don't have chloroplasts, so we can't be "solar powered." But *Elysia chlorotica* found a way around this. They suck out the chloroplasts from the algae they eat and plop them into their own cells. Amazingly, it works. These slugs are now members of a very elite club of photosynthesizing animals.

Most animals can't pluck a body part out of another organism and install it in themselves, so the slug is a bit of a headscratcher to scientists. Even stranger, the chloroplasts are able to produce energy for longer in the slug than they can in the algae. Scientists are still researching these little slugs, but one thing is certain—they make us sandwich-eaters green with envy.

Green About the Gills

The algae give another perk to the sea slugs. They turn the slugs a bright green color, which acts as a camouflage against hungry predators.

Elysia chlorotica consuming its algal food, *Vaucheria litorea*.

Odd Couples Trivia Answer

Gut flora is the name for:

a. all the microorganisms that live in an animal's intestines. (correct)

b. a type of flower that causes stomachaches in humans when eaten.

c. a tiny parasite that replaces the stomach of an organism with its own stomach.

You have a big microbe party going on in your digestive tract, and you wouldn't want it any other way. These microbes help with digestion and play important parts in keeping your digestive system healthy. In fact, the human gut has more than 500 different species of bacteria.

Think About It

All organisms rely on other organisms. Think of your favorite plant or animal. What organisms does it depend on for survival? Write thank you notes from your organism to its "buddies" for all the things they do for it. The goofier and funnier, the better!

Blue milk mushroom

6 Say Hello to My Little Friend

Friends come in all sizes, from big to small to in-between.

You don't have to be 10-feet tall—or any-feet tall—to make a positive impact. In nature, sometimes the most teeny-tiny pal can be the most important. Just ask these organisms how they feel about their "little friends."

Do You Know Your Odd Couples?

This weird fungus attracts flies only to cover them with sticky goo, so it can spread its spores.

a. Octopus stinkhorn fungus

b. Bleeding tooth fungus

c. Blue milk mushroom

Find out the answer at the end of the chapter!

I Hoopoe You Like Bacteria

Hoopoes (WHO-poos or WHO-pose) are pretty birds, with black-and-white banded wings, Mohawk-style head crests, and long, elegant beaks. Hoopoes live throughout Africa, Europe, and Asia. They also have some seriously nasty habits.

Most birds have a "preen gland"—or uropygial (your-oh-PIE-gee-al) gland, scientifically speaking—underneath their tail feathers. The gland produces an oily, waxy substance that birds spread over their bodies as they preen; the goop protects birds' feathers from water and parasites.

Hoopoes have preen glands, too. But they've stepped up the goop game, by hosting colonies of bacteria within those glands. These bacteria add an extra element to the secretions—instead of the usual white color, hoopoe preen gland fluid is dark brown. As a "bonus," it smells like rotting meat. But hoopoes still use their beaks to coat it all over their feathers. Yum.

Why do hoopoes recruit bacteria to spruce up their preen goop? Scientists believe it may have to do with another nasty habit. When a young hoopoe in the nest is threatened, its defense mechanism is to spray a stream of liquid feces at the attacker. Unlike other birds, the hoopoes don't clean this waste—or other waste—out of their nests, leaving themselves at risk for infections. The substances added by the bacteria in their preen glands include chemicals that kill harmful infectious bacteria, including those that can degrade feathers.

Going the Egg-stra Mile

Hoopoes don't just coat themselves in their funky preen fluid—they also bathe their eggs in it. Unlike most bird eggs, hoopoe eggs have tiny pits in the shell, and mama birds slather them with preen juice, which seeps into the pits and protects the developing chicks from infections.

From Breakfast to Besties

Rufous woodpecker
nesting in tree ant nest

Rufous woodpeckers love ants. Mostly when they're hungry—but not always. The woodpeckers live in South Asia and India, and a large part of their diet is ants. That includes a species of "acrobat ants" called *Crematogaster* (cree-mat-oh-GAS-ter), who build large football-shaped nests in the branches of trees. Most of the time, the birds are happy to snack on the ants. And the ants, while probably not "happy" to be eaten, can't really do much about it.

But when Rufous woodpecker nesting season rolls around, the situation changes. Rather than build their own nest, soon-to-be-proud-parent birds will pick out a *Crematogaster* nest and peck a big hole in the side. The female will climb in, lay eggs, and use it as her own nest until the chicks have hatched and are ready to fly on their own.

This might seem awfully rude—adding egg-sult to injury, even. But for putting up with their new tenants, the ants catch a big break: the visiting birds won't eat any of the ants from that nest. Even better, they do their best to keep other peckish woodpeckers away from those ants, too. So the ants get some protection, and in return they don't attack the invading birds, the eggs, or the hatched chicks. It's an odd arrangement for the ants, but it's probably better than winding up as bird food.

An Amazingly Amiable Ant

Crematogaster ants are no strangers to making friends and working with other species. They're among the ants that live in and protect African acacia trees. And some *Crematogaster* species engage in "ranching" or "farming" behavior. They herd groups of small insects like aphids or leafhoppers together, protecting them and feeding on nutrient-rich fluids they produce.

It Pays to Have Friends
With Friends

The citrus mealybug has a problem. Not that it looks like a sugar-dusted skin flake with legs. It does, but mealybugs probably don't care much about looks. Instead, like many creatures—including humans—citrus mealybugs can't make certain amino acids inside their bodies. Amino acids are needed to make proteins, which organisms need to live. So they're kind of important.

Some animals solve this problem by getting amino acids they can't make themselves—sometimes called *essential amino acids*—in their diets. Others have taken the strategy of co-opting bacteria to live in their digestive tracts. If those bacteria can make the amino acids, the host can use them—and the bacteria get lots of food in the meantime. It's a win-win situation.

Citrus mealybugs have gone a step further, creating a win-win-win. The mealybugs host bacteria called *Tremblaya princeps* (trem-BLY-ah PRIN-seps) in their guts, to help them make amino acids. But somewhere along the way, *Tremblaya* picked up a partner—even smaller bacteria called *Moranella endobia* (more-an-ELL-ah en-DOUGH-bee-ah), which live inside it.

This nesting-doll arrangement of cooperating critters is key, because all three organisms now rely on the partnership. The mealybugs can't survive without the amino acids the bacteria produce, and neither bacterial species has enough genes to make everything they need to live, either. It's the only case of friend-in-a-friend-in-another-friend symbiosis known in nature.

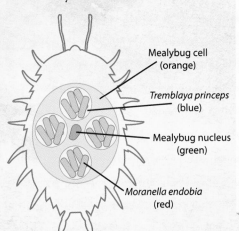

Mealybug cell
(orange)

Tremblaya princeps
(blue)

Mealybug nucleus
(green)

Moranella endobia
(red)

The Ghosts of Pals Past

It isn't just two bacterial species that citrus mealybugs lean on for help. Genetic studies have shown the bugs have "borrowed" genes from three other types of bacteria. Those species may have once also called the mealybugs "home," but all they've left behind is their DNA.

The App-EEL of a Clean Mouth

If you always have people grousing at you to clean up your room, perhaps you'd be better off living under the sea where there are a bunch of teeny maids. Cleaner shrimp are known for setting up little cleaning stations in the sea where sea critters stop by to get cleaned off. It's just like a car wash without the free turtle wax. (Turtles have to pay for cleaning services just like everyone else.)

Cleaner shrimp actually clean off and eat parasites from other sea critters. It's a good deal for both of them—the shrimp gets lunch and the sea animal is free of a pesky little bugger that is causing it harm. When a shrimp is available for service, it dances to attract its next client. (We think this is something that hair salons should adopt. Primping and a dance party? Count us in.)

One of the critters these shrimp service is the moray eel, which actually has quite the taste for crustaceans. You'd think that these eels would lure the shrimp over to eat them, but that doesn't seem to be the case. The eels let the shrimp do their thing and then send them on their way. Maybe they are a little weirded out by a meal that's willing to clean its own dishes.

Cleaning Off the Hollywood Star

Due to their bright red color, Pacific cleaner shrimp are very popular aquarium pets. Not to mention, at least one of them is a celebrity. Jacques, the shrimp from *Finding Nemo*, is a cleaner shrimp. It is still unknown whether cleaner shrimp actually speak in French accents when we're not listening.

Rise and Shine
(and Shine and Shine)

A friend is always there when you need him, and that's definitely true for the bobtail squid and its bacterial buddies. This squid keeps a nest of bioluminescent bacteria in its belly that make the squid glow in the dark. The bacteria get food from the squid and in turn, they protect the squid from predators. Their glow prevents the squid from making a shadow, so hungry sea critters swimming below can't see the squid swimming above them. It's an underwater invisibility cloak that would even make Harry Potter jealous.

Oddly, the bacteria might even control when the squids sleep. Humans are hard-wired to sleep at night due to our circadian rhythm, which is a bit like an internal alarm clock. Our bodies respond to the amount of light around us, secreting sleepy chemicals when it's dark and wake-up-sleepyhead chemicals during the day. Scientists recently found that the light from the bacteria may affect the squid's circadian rhythm. Though this shouldn't be surprising. When you have a sleepover with millions of friends waving glow sticks, your beauty sleep is bound to be interrupted.

Never Overstay Your Welcome

Despite the benefit they provide, the squids don't keep their glowing bacteria inside of them permanently. During the day, they eject almost all of the bacteria out, which is a response to sunlight. At night, their bacterial buddies creep back in, allowing for the late-night tentacle-laden light show.

Octopus stinkhorn fungus

Odd Couples Trivia Answer

This weird fungus attracts flies only to cover them with sticky goo, so it can spread its spores.

a. Octopus stinkhorn fungus (correct)
b. Bleeding tooth fungus
c. Blue milk mushroom

The octopus stinkhorn fungus is a scary-looking organism, indeed. It grows long red "tentacles" which release a foul smell that attracts flies and other stink-loving insects. When the flies land on it, they get covered with the fungus's sticky spores. Wherever the spores fall off, a new creepy tentacle-sprouting fungus may grow.

Think About It

You are never alone—literally. Inside and outside your body, you have billions of microscopic organisms helping you carry out your life functions. What do you think we'd look like if we could actually see all of the "little friends" we have living on (and in, and off of) us? Research the microbes living on or in the human body and draw a picture of yourself with all of your little microbe friends!

Mosquito

Bibliography

Introduction

Biology4Kids.com. (n.d.). *Relationships between organisms*. Retrieved from http://www.biology4kids.com/files/studies_relationships.html

Grabianowski, E. (2008). How symbiosis works. *How Stuff Works*. Retrieved from http://science.howstuffworks.com/life/evolution/symbiosis.htm

Nguyen, D. H. (2016). Five types of ecological relationships. *Seattlepi*. Retrieved from http://education.seattlepi.com/five-types-ecological-relationships-4019.html

Chapter 1

Peculiar Pals

BBC One. (2016). *Nature's greatest dancers–Pom pom crab*. Retrieved from http://www.bbc.co.uk/programmes/articles/jM428XVv2m8mXWFB3HCLGL/pom-pom-crab

Crowther, A. L. (n.d.). Invertebrate of the month. *Florida Museum of Natural History*. Retrieved from https://www.flmnh.ufl.edu/malacology/invert.htm

Dorippe frascone. (n.d.). *ZipcodeZoo*. Retrieved from http://zipcodezoo.com/index.php/Dorippe_frascone

Drake, N. (2015). Scientists uncover strange secret life of a jungle butterfly. *National Geographic*. Retrieved from http://news.nationalgeographic.com/2015/12/151203-caterpillar-ant-parasitic-plant-Peru-science-evolution

Ghose, T. (2015a). Gorgeous images reveal parasitic plant in 3-way symbiotic relationship. *LiveScience.* Retrieved from http://www.livescience.com/532 30-ant-caterpillar-parasite-relationship.html

Ghose, T. (2015b) Photos: A strange parasitic plant in the Amazon. *LiveScience.* Retrieved from http://www.livescience.com/53229-parasitic-plant-ant-cater pillar.html

Heart urchin pea crab, red heart sea urchin [Weblog post]. (2012). Retrieved from http://www.coralreefphotos.com/heart-urchin-pea-crab-red-heart-sea-urchin

Kaplan, E. H. (1982). *A field guide to coral reefs: Caribbean and Florida* [Google books version]. Retrieved from https://books.google.com/books?id=OLYPWMoBkcc C&pg=PA242&lpg=PA242&dq=urchin+crab+symbiosis&source=bl&ots=1Ud 3wJVzdU&sig=I7p6Q_KP7XxzrHIc4t7bSHIPuAA&hl=en&sa=X&ved=0ahU KEwicm4GlqtPLAhVENhoKHVRbDi84HhDoAQg1MAQ#v=onepage&q= urchin%20crab%20symbiosis&f=false

Kovner, A. (2015). Ménage à trois in the Amazon. *Sierra Club.* Retrieved from http://www.sierraclub.org/sierra/2016-1-january-february/green-life/m-nage-trois-amazon

Mystery of the yellow bulbs: Discovery of a new caterpillar-ant-parasitic plant relationship [Weblog post]. (2015). Retrieved from http://blog.perunature.com/2015/11/mystery-of-yellow-bulbs-discovery-of.html

NAD-Lembeh. (n.d.). *Carrier crabs* [Weblog post]. Retrieved from http://www.nad-lembeh.com/blog/uncategorized/1149/carrier-crabs

Pappas, S. (2015). How hungry pitcher plants get the poop they need. *LiveScience.* Retrieved from http://www.livescience.com/51501-pitcher-plants-lure-pooping-bats.html

Scharmann, M., Thornham, D., Grafe, T., & Federle, W. (2013). A novel type of nutritional ant–plant interaction: Ant partners of carnivorous pitcher plants prevent nutrient export by Dipteran Pitcher Infauna. *PLOS ONE, 8*(5), e63556. doi: 10.1371/journal.pone.0063556

Symbiotic relationships within the reef [Weblog post]. (n.d.). Retrieved from http://thegreatbarrierreef1.weebly.com/symbiotic-relationships.html

Thompson, H. (2014). What drives a sloth's ritualistic trek to poop? *Smithsonian Magazine*. Retrieved from http://www.smithsonianmag.com/articles/what-drives-a-sloths-ritualistic-trek-to-poop-180949419/?no-ist

Viegas, J. (2011). Bat uses carnivorous plant as a toilet. *Discovery News*. Retrieved from http://news.discovery.com/animals/zoo-animals/bat-carnivorous-plant-bathroom-110125.htm

Weis, J. S. (2012). *Walking sideways: The remarkable world of crabs* [Googlebooks version]. Retrieved from https://books.google.com/books?id=q8QBYtvmpcAC&pg=PA121&lpg=PA121&dq=%2B%22urchin+crab%22&source=bl&ots=qD5i4Rc_0v&sig=PLd_pbswGjzKptGjMF6Uip8Mj0c&hl=en&sa=X&ved=0ahUKEwj7v6m3ptPLAhXKHB4KHfLUD1Y4ChDoAQg5MAU#v=onepage&q&f=false

Yong, E. (2014). Can moths explain why sloths poo on the ground? *National Geographic*. Retrieved from http://phenomena.nationalgeographic.com/2014/01/21/can-moths-explain-why-sloths-poo-on-the-ground

Chapter 2

Give and Take (But Mostly Take)

Adams, R., Liberti, J., Illum, A., Jones, T., Nash, D., & Boomsma, J. (2013). Chemically armed mercenary ants protect fungus-farming societies. *Proceedings of the National Academy of Sciences, 110,* 15752–15757. Retrieved from http://www.pnas.org/content/110/39/15752

Armitage, H. (2015). Tapeworms may be good for your brain. *Science*. Retrieved from http://www.sciencemag.org/news/2015/08/tapeworms-may-be-good-your-brain

Bruzek, A. (2014). Drugged marshmallows can keep urban raccoons from spreading disease. *NPR*. Retrieved from http://www.npr.org/sections/health-shots/2014/11/25/366333890/drugged-marshmallows-can-keep-urban-raccoons-from-spreading-disease

Gavin, P., Kazacos, K., & Shulman, S. (2005). Baylisascariasis. *Clinical Microbiology Reviews, 18,* 703–718. Retrieved from http://dx.doi.org/10.1128/cmr.18.4.703–718.2005

Gill, A., Darby, A., & Makepeace, B. (2014). Iron necessity: The secret of Wolbachia's success? *PLOS Neglected Tropical Diseases, 8*(10), e3224. Retrieved from http://dx.doi.org/10.1371/journal.pntd.0003224

Haider, S., Khairnar, K., Martin, D., Yang, J., Ralevski, F., Kazacos, K., & Pillai, D. (2012). Possible pet-associated Baylisascariasis in child, Canada. *Emerging Infectious Diseases, 18,* 347–349. Retrieved from http://dx.doi.org/10.3201/eid1802.110674

Herasimtschuk, D. (2010). A Pacific chorus frog with limb deformities caused by parasite infection, pictured in a studio in 2010 [Photo]. *National Geographic.* Retrieved from http://news.nationalgeographic.com/news/2011/08/110802-frogs-deformed-parasites-animals-environment-mutants

Hurd, H., Warr, E., & Polwart, A. (2001). A parasite that increases host lifespan. *Proceedings of the Royal Society B: Biological Sciences, 268,* 1749–1753. Retrieved from http://rspb.royalsocietypublishing.org/content/268/1477/1749

The Johnson Lab—UC at Boulder. (2015). *Amphibian malformations.* Retrieved from http://www.colorado.edu/eeb/facultysites/pieter/amphibianmalformations.html

Johnson, P. (2003). Amphibian deformities and Ribeiroia infection: an emerging helminthiasis. *Trends in Parasitology, 19,* 332–335. Retrieved from http://dx.doi.org/10.1016/s1471-4922(03)00148-x

Kaplan, M. (2011). Healthy horrors: The benefits of parasites. *Science in School.* Retrieved from http://www.scienceinschool.org/2011/issue20/horrors

Kremer, N., Charif, D., Henri, H., Bataille, M., Prévost, G., Kraaijeveld, K., & Vavre, F. (2009). A new case of Wolbachia dependence in the genus Asobara: Evidence for parthenogenesis induction in Asobara japonica. *Heredity, 103,* 248–256. Retrieved from http://dx.doi.org/10.1038/hdy.2009.63

Kremer, N., Dedeine, F., Charif, D., Finet, C., Allemand, R., & Vavre, F. (2010). Do variable compensatory mechanisms explain the polymorphism of the dependence phenotype in the Asobara tabida-Wolbachia association? *Evolution, 64,* 2969–

2979. Retrieved from http://www.jstor.org/stable/40863387?seq=1#page_scan_tab_contents

Main, D. (2014). Leishmania parasite: Deadly for humans, but good for flies? *Popular Science*. Retrieved from http://www.popsci.com/article/science/leishmania-parasite-deadly-humans-good-flies

Michigan Department of Natural Resources. (2016). *DNR—Raccoon roundworm (Baylisascaris)*. Retrieved from https://www.michigan.gov/dnr/0,4570,7-153-103 70_12150_12220-27261--,00.html

Moreira, L. A., Iturbe-Ormaetxe, I., Jeffery, J. A., Lu, G., Pyke, A. T., Hedges, L. M., . . . O'Neill, S. L. (2009). A Wolbachia symbiont in Aedes aegypti limits infection with Dengue, Chikungunya, and Plasmodium. *Cell, 139,* 1268–1278. doi: 10.1016/j.cell.2009.11.042

O'Neill, S. (2015). The dengue stopper. *Scientific American, 312*(6), 72–77. Retrieved from http://www.nature.com/scientificamerican/journal/v312/n6/full/scientific american0615-72.html

Pieter T. J., Lunde, K. B., Thurman, E. M., Ritchie, E. G., Wray, S. N., Sutherland, D. R., . . . Blaustein, A. R. (2002). Parasite (Ribeiroia ondatrae) infection linked to amphibian malformations in the Western United States. *Ecological Monographs, 72,* 151–168. Retrieved from http://www.jstor.org/stable/3100022?seq=1#page_scan_tab_contents

Sirucek, S. (2013). Enemies with benefits: How parasitic ants protect their hosts. *National Geographic*. Retrieved from http://voices.nationalgeographic.com/2013/09/14/enemies-with-benefits-how-parasitic-ants-protect-their-hosts

Tapeworm. (2016). In *The Columbia Encyclopedia* (6th ed.). Retrieved from http://www.encyclopedia.com/topic/Tapeworms.aspx

Timmermans, M., & Ellers, J. (2009). Wolbachia endosymbiont is essential for egg hatching in a parthenogenetic arthropod. *Evolutionary Ecology*. Retrieved from http://agris.fao.org/agris-search/search.do?recordID=US201301706011

Wildlife disease—Raccoon roundworm. (2016). *Nwco.net*. Retrieved from http://nwco.net/044-wildlifediseases

Chapter 3

May I Have This Dance?

Animal Corner. (n.d.). *Galapagos great frigate bird.* Retrieved from https://animalcorner.co.uk/animals/galapagos-great-frigate-bird

Arnold, C. (2015). Behold Sparklemuffin and Skeletorus, new peacock spiders. *National Geographic.* Retrieved from http://news.nationalgeographic.com/2015/03/150324-australia-peacock-spider-sparklemuffin-new-species

Banwell, H. (2009). Courtship of the magnificent frigatebird. *Bird Ecology Study Group.* Retrieved from http://www.besgroup.org/2009/03/17/courtship-of-the-magnificent-frigatebird

Cornell Lab—Bird Academy. (2010). *Inflatable throat: magnificent Frigatebird mating display* [Video file]. Retrieved from https://academy.allaboutbirds.org/an-inflatable-throat-magnificent-frigatebird-mating-display

Crew, B. (2014). New species of peacock spider has leopard spots and cat-like moves. *Scientific American.* Retrieved from http://blogs.scientificamerican.com/running-ponies/new-species-of-peacock-spider-has-leopard-spots-and-cat-like-moves

Hiskey, D. (2012). The male white-fronted parrot vomits in the female's mouth during their mating ritual. *Today I Found Out.* Retrieved from http://www.todayifoundout.com/index.php/2012/09/the-male-white-fronted-parrot-vomits-in-the-females-mouth-during-their-mating-ritual

Hooded Seals, Cystophora cristata. (n.d.). *MarineBio.* Retrieved from http://marinebio.org/species.asp?id=304

Jankowiak, W., Volsche, S., & Garcia, J. (2015). Is the romantic-sexual kiss a near human universal? *American Anthropologist, 117,* 535–539. Retrieved from http://dx.doi.org/10.1111/aman.12286

Lin, S. (2014). Tiny coqui frog becomes a big problem in Hawaii. *Los Angeles Times.* Retrieved from http://www.latimes.com/nation/la-na-coqui-frog-hawaii-20141228-story.html

Morell, V. (2010). Bowerbirds. *National Geographic*. Retrieved from http://ngm. nationalgeographic.com/2010/07/bowerbirds/morell-text

Moskvitch, K. (2014). Urban frogs use drains as mating megaphones. *Nature*. Retrieved from http://dx.doi.org/10.1038/nature.2014.15362

National Geographic. (n.d.). *World's weirdest: Birds "moonwalk" to impress the ladies* [Video file]. Retrieved from http://video.nationalgeographic.com/video/weirdest-manakin-dance

National Geographic. (n.d.) *World's weirdest: Bowerbird woos female with ring* [Video file]. Retrieved from http://video.nationalgeographic.com/video/weirdest-bowerbird

PBS Nature. (2008). *Animal antics quiz answers*. Retrieved from http://www.pbs.org/wnet/nature/what-males-will-do-animal-antics-quiz-answers/949

Scully, S. (2014). Love, naturally. *Audubon*. Retrieved from https://www.audubon.org/news/love-naturally

UW-Milwaukee Field Station. (n.d.). *Red velvet mite*. Retrieved from https://www4.uwm.edu/fieldstation/naturalhistory/bugoftheweek/red_velvet_mite.cfm

Viegas, J. (2014). Frog uses drainpipe to amp up mating calls. *Discovery News*. Retrieved from http://news.discovery.com/animals/endangered-species/frog-croons-in-drainpipe-to-amp-up-mating-calls-140604.htm

White-fronted Amazon. (2016). *Parrots wikia*. Retrieved from http://parrots.wikia.com/wiki/White-fronted_Amazon

Chapter 4

Deadly Duos

Baker, A., Mutton, T., Hines, H., & Dyck, S. (2014). The Black-tailed Antechinus, Antechinus arktos sp. nov.: A new species of carnivorous marsupial from montane regions of the Tweed Volcano caldera, eastern Australia. *Zootaxa, 3765*(2), 101. Retrieved from http://dx.doi.org/10.11646/zootaxa.3765.2.1

Bryner, J. (2009). Sneaky spider skips long sex dance. *LiveScience*. Retrieved from http://www.livescience.com/9759-sneaky-spider-skips-long-sex-dance.html

Chase, R. (2007). The function of dart shooting in helicid snails. *American Melacological Bulletin*. Retrieved from http://www.bioone.org/doi/abs/10.4003/0740-2783-23.1.183

Chase, R., & Blanchard, K. (2006). The snail's love-dart delivers mucus to increase paternity. *Proceedings of the Royal Society B: Biological Sciences, 273*, 1471–1475. http://dx.doi.org/10.1098/rspb.2006.3474

Deutschmann, J. (2015). Marsupials mating: Antechinus mass die off linked to suicidal sex ritual. *The Inquisitr*. Retrieved from http://www.inquisitr.com/2138177/marsupials-mating-2

Dolgin, E. (2009). Lazy male spiders avoid dinner date. *Nature*. Retrieved from http://www.nature.com/news/2009/091021/full/news.2009.1020.html

Encyclopedia Britannica. (n.d.). *Fig wasp*. Retrieved from http://www.britannica.com/animal/fig-wasp

Fiegl, A. (2009). Fresh figs, and bugs? *Smithsonian Magazine*. Retrieved from http://www.smithsonianmag.com/arts-culture/fresh-figs-and-bugs-66202233/?no-ist

Geggel, L. (2015). Suicidal sexcapades: 2 newfound marsupials do it to death. *LiveScience*. Retrieved from http://www.livescience.com/51059-new-marsupials-antechinus.html

Houston, T. (2011). Dawson's burrowing bee (Amegilla dawsoni). *Western Australian Museum*. Retrieved from http://museum.wa.gov.au/research/collections/terrestrial-zoology/entomology-insect-collection/entomology-factsheets/dawsons-burrowing-bee

Koene, J., & Schulenburg, H. (2005). Shooting darts: Co-evolution and counter-adaptation in hermaphroditic snails. *BMC Evolutionary Biology 5*(1), 25. Retrieved from http://bmcevolbiol.biomedcentral.com/articles/10.1186/1471-2148-5-25

Landolfa, M. (2001). Dart shooting influences paternal reproductive success in the snail Helix aspersa (Pulmonata, Stylommatophora). *Behavioral Ecology, 12*, 773–777.

MacDonald, F. (2015). Scientists find two new marsupial species that mate themselves to death. *ScienceAlert*. Retrieved from http://www.sciencealert.com/scientists-find-new-species-of-marsupial-that-mate-themselves-to-death

Martins, R. (2015). Love hurts: What happens when snails stab their mates. *National Geographic*. Retrieved from http://news.nationalgeographic.com/2015/03/1503 10-snails-reproduction-sex-animals-science-evolution

Nearhos, P. (2010). *BBC LIFE—Dawson's bees*. [Video file]. Retrieved from https://www.youtube.com/watch?v=mtpECWl-5v4

Simmons, L., Tomkins, J., & Alcock, J. (2000). Can minor males of Dawson's burrowing bee, Amegilla dawsoni (Hymenoptera: Anthophorini) compensate for reduced access to virgin females through sperm competition? *Behavioral Ecology, 11*, 319–325. http://dx.doi.org/10.1093/beheco/11.3.319

Stoltz, J., Elias, D., & Andrade, M. (2008). Females reward courtship by competing males in a cannibalistic spider. *Behavioral Ecology Sociobiology, 62*, 689–697. Retrieved from http://nature.berkeley.edu/eliaslab/Publications/StoltzEtAl2008a.pdf

Stoltz, J., Elias, D., & Andrade, M. (2009). Male courtship effort determines female response to competing rivals in redback spiders. *Animal Behaviour, 77*, 79–85. Retrieved from http://nature.berkeley.edu/eliaslab/Publications/StoltzEtAl2009a.pdf

Viegas, J. (2009). Deadly spider requires long courtship—or else. *Discovery News*. Retrieved from http://www.nbcnews.com/id/33422436/ns/technology_and_science-science/t/deadly-spider-requires-long-courtship-or-else/#.VwcMBfkrKCj

Walker, M. (2009). Bees fight to death over females. *BBC Earth News*. Retrieved from http://news.bbc.co.uk/earth/hi/earth_news/newsid_8354000/8354788.stm

Chapter 5

You Complete Me

Acacia-ant mutualism? [Weblog post]. (2012). *AntBlog.* Retrieved from http://www.antweb.org/antblog/2012/11/acacia-ant-mutualism.html

Ainsworth, C. (2003). The stranger within. *New Scientist.* Retrieved from https://www.newscientist.com/article/mg18024215-100-the-stranger-within

Bungartz, F. (n.d.). An overview on the biology of lichens. *Arizona State University Lichen Herbarium.* Retrieved from http://nhc.asu.edu/lherbarium/lichen_info

Clemens, D. (2015). Captivating blue dragon sea slug washes up in Australia. *Discovery News.* Retrieved from http://news.discovery.com/animals/captivating-blue-dragon-sea-slug-washes-up-in-australia-151123.htm

Encyclopedia Britannica. (n.d.) *Portuguese man-of-war.* Retrieved from http://www.britannica.com/animal/Portuguese-man-of-war

Heil, M., Barajas-Barron, A., Orona-Tamayo, D., Wielsch, N., & Svatos, A. (2013). Partner manipulation stabilises a horizontally transmitted mutualism. *Ecology Letters, 17*(2), 185–192. Retrieved from http://dx.doi.org/10.1111/ele.12215

Holdrege, C. (2008). Ants, acacias and herbivores. *The Nature Institute.* Retrieved from http://natureinstitute.org/pub/ic/ic20/ants.htm

Kenney, D. (2015). Sea slug has taken genes from the algae it eats, allowing it to photosynthesize like a plant, study reports. *Marine Biological Library.* Retrieved from http://blog.mbl.edu/?p=3285

Lichens are fungi! (n.d.). Retrieved from http://herbarium.usu.edu/fungi/funfacts/lichens.htm

Lichen biology and the environment. (n.d.). Retrieved from http://www.lichen.com/biology.html

Malakoff, D. (2014). Half-male, half-female bird has a rough life. *Science.* Retrieved from http://www.sciencemag.org/news/2014/12/half-male-half-female-bird-has-rough-life

Max Planck Institute for Chemical Ecology. (2014). Ants protect acacia plants against pathogens. *Science Daily*. Retrieved from https://www.sciencedaily.com/releases/2014/01/140115113243.htm

Mosaicism and chimerism. (n.d.). Retrieved from http://www.vivo.colostate.edu/hbooks/genetics/medgen/chromo/mosaics.html

National Geographic. (n.d.). *Portuguese man-of-war* [Video file]. Retrieved from http://video.nationalgeographic.com/video/manowar_portuguese

National Geographic. (n.d.). *Portuguese man-of-war* [Photographs]. Retrieved from http://animals.nationalgeographic.com/animals/invertebrates/portuguese-man-of-war

National Geographic. (2012). *World's weirdest—Portuguese man-of-war* [Video file]. Retrieved from https://www.youtube.com/watch?v=xTgLTbXJrfM

Rybak, S. (2013). 4 incredible photosynthetic animals. *Uloop*. Retrieved from http://umich.uloop.com/news/view.php/77109/4-incredible-photosynthetic-animals

Yong, E. (2013). Trees trap ants into sweet servitude. *National Geographic*. Retrieved from http://news.nationalgeographic.com/news/2013/11/131106-ants-tree-acacia-food-mutualism

Yuan, X., Xiao, S., & Taylor, T. N. (2005). Lichen-like symbiosis 600 million years ago. *Science, 308,* 1017–1020. Retrieved from http://dx.doi.org/10.1126/science.1111347

Chapter 6

Say Hello to My Little Friend

Becker, J., Curtis, L., & Grutter, A. (2005). Cleaner shrimp use a rocking dance to advertise cleaning service to clients. *Current Biology, 15,* 760–764. Retrieved from http://dx.doi.org/10.1016/j.cub.2005.02.067

Chong, K. W. (2013). Nest of the Rufous woodpecker. *Bird Ecology Study Group*. Retrieved from http://www.besgroup.org/2013/09/14/nest-of-the-rufous-woodpecker

Crematogaster (acrobat ant). (2016). Retrieved from http://www.tightloop.com/ants/crespp.htm

Eveleth, R. (2013). Bacteria makes squid sparkly and sleepy. *Smithsonian Magazine*. Retrieved from http://www.smithsonianmag.com/smart-news/bacteria-makes-squid-sparkly-and-sleepy-39516

Frazer, J. (2011). Cow-like mealybug home to sexy symbiotic machine. *Scientific American*. Retrieved from http://blogs.scientificamerican.com/artful-amoeba/cow-like-mealybug-home-to-sexy-symbiotic-machine

Grice, E., Kong, H., Conlan, S., Deming, C., Davis, J., Young, A., . . . Segre, J. (2009). Topographical and temporal diversity of the human skin microbiome. *Science, 324,* 1190–1192. Retrieved from http://dx.doi.org/10.1126/science.1171700

Heath-Heckman, E., Peyer, S., Whistler, C., Apicella, M., Goldman, W., & McFall-Ngai, M. (2013). Bacterial bioluminescence regulates expression of a host cryptochrome gene in the squid-vibrio symbiosis. *mBio, 4*(2), e00167-13. Retrieved from http://dx.doi.org/10.1128/mbio.00167-13

Husnik, F., Nikoh, N., Koga, R., Ross, L., Duncan, R., Fujie, M., . . . McCutheon, J. P. (2013). Horizontal gene transfer from diverse bacteria to an insect genome enables a tripartite nested mealybug symbiosis. *Cell, 153,* 1567–1578. Retrieved from http://dx.doi.org/10.1016/j.cell.2013.05.040

India Biodiversity Portal. (n.d.). *Celeus brachyurus (Vieillot, 1818)*. Retrieved from http://indiabiodiversity.org/species/show/33875

Kew Royal Botanical Gardens. (n.d.). *Clathrus archeri (devil's fingers)*. Retrieved from http://www.kew.org/science-conservation/plants-fungi/clathrus-archeri-devils-fingers

O'Brien, M. (2010). Shining symbiosis: Bobtail squid and their bacteria buddies. *Phys.org*. Retrieved from http://phys.org/news/2010-11-symbiosis-bobtail-squid-bacteria-buddies.html

Rodríguez-Ruano, S., Martín-Vivaldi, M., Martín-Platero, A., López-López, J., Peralta-Sánchez, J., Ruiz-Rodríguez, M., . . . Martínez-Bueno, M. (2015). The hoopoe's uropygial gland hosts a bacterial community influenced by the living conditions of the bird. *PLOS One, 10*(10), e0139734. Retrieved from http://dx.doi.org/10.1371/journal.pone.0139734

Schaeter, M. (2009). Bacteria of a feather . . . [Weblog post]. *Small Things Considered.* Retrieved from http://schaechter.asmblog.org/schaechter/2009/12/ba.html

Wilkins, A. (2011). The ultimate symbiosis: Mealybugs have bacteria living inside their bacteria. *Io9.* Retrieved from http://io9.gizmodo.com/5830671/the-ultimate-symbiosis-mealybugs-have-bacteria-living-inside-their-bacteria

World Association of Zoos and Aquariums. (n.d.). *Pacific cleaner shrimp (Lysmata amboinensi).* Retrieved from http://www.waza.org/en/zoo/choose-a-species/invertebrates/other-aquatic-invertebrates/lysmata-amboinensis

Vishnudas, C. (2008). Crematogaster ants in shaded coffee plantations: a critical food source for Rufous woodpecker Micropternus brachyurus and other forest birds. *ResearchGate.* Retrieved from https://www.researchgate.net/publication/242173919_Crematogaster_ants_in_shaded_coffee_plantations_a_critical_food_source_for_Rufous_Woodpecker_Micropternus_brachyurus_and_other_forest_birds

Yong, E. (2013). Snug as a bug in a bug in a bug. *National Geographic.* Retrieved from http://phenomena.nationalgeographic.com/2013/06/20/snug-as-a-bug-in-a-bug-in-a-bug

Yong, E. (2014). The bird that paints its eggs with bacteria. *National Geographic.* Retrieved from http://phenomena.nationalgeographic.com/2014/06/27/the-bird-that-paints-its-eggs-with-bacteria

Zielinski, S. (2009). Bacteria help a funny-looking bird, the hoopoe. *Smithsonian Magazine.* Retrieved from http://www.smithsonianmag.com/science-nature/bacteria-help-a-funny-looking-bird-the-hoopoe-18494692

Water buffalo

Oxpecker

About the Authors

Jenn and Charlie are Boston-based science nerds who met through stand-up comedy. By day, Jenn writes science textbooks and Charlie slings data for a cancer research company. By night, they make comedy films and stay up past their bedtime e-mailing pictures of weird animals to each other.

Lovebirds

Image Credits

The publisher would like to thank the following for their permission to reproduce their images:

Cover: Jürgen C. Otto (top right); Page ii: James Steinberg/Science Source; Page iv: Reinhard Dirscherl/Alamy Stock Photo; Page 6 and 7: Merlin D. Tuttle/Science Source; Page 8: David Fleetham/Alamy Stock Photo; Page 12: Georgette Douwma/Science Source; Page 13: Steve Jones; Page 14 and 15: Aaron Pomerantz/PeruNature.com; Page 16: Mark Moffett/Minden Pictures; Page 21: William J. Murray/Clinical Infectious Diseases; Page 22: Brett A. Goodman and Pieter T. J. Johnson; Page 23: Anand Varma/National Geographic Creative; Page 25: Zhiyong Xi/Michigan State University; Page 26 and 27: Alex Wild; Page 28: Biophoto Associates/Science Source; Page 30: Scott Camazine/Alamy Stock Photo; Page 34 and 35: Jürgen C. Otto; Page 36: Yung-chieh Lin; Page 41: M. Watson/Science Source; Page 48: Danita Delimont/Alamy Stock Photo; Page 49: Universal Images Group North America LLC/Alamy Stock Photo; Page 50: Bernhard Jacobi; Page 51: Bill Bachman/Alamy Stock Photo; Page 54: B.G. Thomson/Science Source; Page 63: Biophoto Associates/Science Source; Page 64: VenusTheAmazingChimeraCat/Facebook; Page 65: Chi Lui/National Geographic; Page 67: WILDLIFE GmbH/Alamy Stock Photo; Page 68: Aaron Ansarov; Page 70: Nicholas E. Curtis and Ray Martinez/University of South Florida; Page 71: Karen N. Pelletreau/University of Connecticut; Page 78: FLPA/Alamy Stock Photo; Page 80: Nigel Cattlin/Science Source